T0198805

Distant Lands and Near

Mark Anthony Signorelli

Trafford rev. 08/02/2012

 www.trafford.com

North America & international
toll-free: 1 888 232 4444 (USA & Canada)
phone: 250 383 6864 ♦ fax: 812 355 4082

Dedicated to my mother,
who first gave me the gift of good words.

The Voyage of Diego Mendez

In naked Jamaica, Columbus' last crew
Sat in extremest enervation
By the side of their ocean-battered ship—
Struck there in helpless dilapidation—
And cast their eyes on the volatile sea
Where they looked for death and not salvation.

Then Diego Mendez rose and he said:
"I will cross the forty leagues of the sea
To Hispaniola, and bring us help
From the men of the Spanish colony;
And I trust for the goodness of the attempt
That our gracious lord will favor me."

So he gathered Flisco, his old friend,
And a few of the sailors fortified
Against the perils of such a task,
And some Arawak, to serve as a guide;
Then they all set out in two canoes
That could barely float above the tide.

The sea swelled flat and tranquilly
Like a plate of blue suspiring glass;
The immoderate sun burned painfully,
Unveiled by a single cloud's thin mass;
And the tangible breeze that stirred at times
Smelled thick with mangrove and sassafras.

But the ocean current under their boats
Ran steady and strongly against their head,
So they pulled at the oars the seering day
Till their palms hard creases blistered and bled—
All day and all night, and when morning came
One man from the strain of it all lay dead.

For two more days and for two more nights,
Across the forty leagues of the sea,
They pulled for Hispaniola's coast
Which their faint eyes searched out desperately,
And two more died, and the others looked
On their quiet cheeks with jealousy.

Still, on they toiled, these fugitive men,
To one another so little known,
With little more language fit to commune
Than a weary and labor-wrested groan,
Or the misery drawn on each taut cheek
That reflected to every man his own;

Cast suddenly in the midst of a sphere
Unknown to them, and unknowable;
Uncertain of how to find their bearing
On a trek momentous and wonderful
Through a natural frame of things at once
Gorgeous and adversarial;

In constant terror of ruinous storms
Arising upon them unaware;
In constant reliance on other's strength—
Both strangers and friends—to get anywhere;
Fatigued to a soul-deep lassitude,
Surrounded by death, beset by despair.

Yet whatever they lacked in that arduous course
They were not deprived a mind assured
Of its righteous aims, nor a tested arm,
To every trial at sea inured,
Nor a spirit in every season inclined
At all pains to do the will of their lord;

And certain it is, whatever the cause,
Whatever the source of that tendency,
And whatever it meant in the final word,
Those little boats and their company
Were the only thing in that mystical realm
That moved against the prevailing sea.

At last the distorted shape of the moon
Gave evidence of the solid shore;
So revivified, they plied at the wave
With a vigor drawn from hope's last store.
At dawn they made land, and the natives came
To greet and to succor the exhausted corps.

They brought many fruits, and spirits to drink,
And garments woven white for this band
That had struggled so long and with such good cause,
Then they lay them down on the night-cooled sand,
Where there was no fear of the sudden gale,
Neither labor, nor heat of the sun to withstand.

Kierkegaard and Regina Meet a Final Time

"God keep you," she said, and nervously paused before him—
She had been his betrothed and beloved, let her heart adore him
Without restraint, but that was before the day
He abandoned her to pursue in his singular way
The truth of things, and bring profit to all mankind
By the sum of his writings—at least, so it seemed to his mind.
Now she stood before this man for a final time
On the eve of her parting into the foreign clime
Of the Caribbean, and he, he eyed her with wonder
As the glow from the gas-lamp fell on her cheek and under
The raven curls that unfolded along her shoulder—
No less fair was that face, though some twenty winters older
Than when it had leaned against his own young cheek—
He fumbled his hat, and vainly struggled to speak;
He desired to say how sorry he was for the act
That hurt her, how sure he was at the time of the fact
That he acted with virtue, that sometimes he seemed to hear
Some strange voice out of heaven—not often heard in this sphere—
That told him he must forget and forfeit all
Of his joy in this world if he would be true to the call
Of his Master, and serve his duty adequately;
But also he wanted to say that he loved her greatly,
That since that time not a day—not an hour—went by
But some vision of her and her grace would occupy
His memory, that often he paused and wondered how life

Would have past, with what peace, had he taken her then for his wife,
And as often he wondered whether indeed he had made
The nobler decision, but Time went by, and had laid
Her petrifying hand on that distant choice.
Regina looked up at him, and attempted to voice
The unclear emotions troubling the well of her soul—
She wanted to say she forgave him the deed and the dole
It had caused her in youth—though she never could comprehend
The hard pilgrimage he made of his life, in the end
She knew he did all to serve God in the best of his light,
And that she, a young girl, and naïve—however she might
Rebel at the truth—she could never expect that her beauty
Could impose on his heart an equally binding duty
As the heavens oblige, but that still remembrance had kept
A place of affection for him, and sometimes she wept
When she thought of his gentle ways, as she wept when young.
So she wanted to speak, but the words would not form on her tongue,
And she only stood restless before him, shy, and repeating
The very words she had barely whispered in greeting:
"God keep you," she said, "and may all go well with you."
Soren was paralyzed with sorrow all through,
And could only manage to make an awkward bow
And walk on, though with heavy and hesitant shuffle, and now
The ambient light of the gas-lamp glows thin on a street
That is empty, as round the corner the sound of her feet
Fades away, and he, he climbs the ill-lit stairs
That lead to his studious chambers, and all that he hears
Is the harsh, distinct noise of his steps as they fall
On the wood, and reverberate through the silent hall.

Tamahay the Sioux

Tamahay the Sioux, a fearsome youth,
    Stood tall as a mountain peak,
And he raised his voice for the gods to hear
    Beside the icy creek:

"If you love me, then let me die young
    Upon the field of war,
And lie where all my foes lie slain,
    As my fathers died before.

For what are all the hopes of life
    But a total waste of breath?
Little has life to offer a man
    But an early and noble death.

Let me die young and glorious,
    Let my flesh lie lifeless and rotten,
But let the Northlands sink in the sea
    When Tamahay is forgotten."

In daring he outdid the hawk,
    And the bear in awesome girth,
And in fame young Tamahay surpassed
    All men upon the earth.

And when the Indian lauded the braves
    Who shone in the dizzy fray,
Always the first to spring from the tongue
    Was the name of Tamahay.

As often in battle, at ease he won
   The hearts of the maiden Sioux,
And many a virgin Tamahay loved—
   Such as young men like to do.

Then the white-man to the Northlands came,
   And he proved a wicked snare,
Stealing the lands the Sioux had roamed
   Since the Father placed them there,

And they threw young Tamahay in prison,
   His arms with shackles piled,
And threatened him with a horrid death,
   But the warrior only smiled.

Now Tamahay, with his wild youth fled,
   Grew tired of the warring life,
And longed for the joys of quiet love,
   And so he took a wife,-

His heart with gentle fondness swelled
   While his wife lay by his side,
And many a year in faith they lived,
   But her heart was flesh, so she died.

Then Tamahay, his fighting soul calmed,
   The adverse white-man befriended,
Led him with careful hand to his home,
   And his raging hunger attended;

And for this, like a common criminal,
   He was cast from his native kin,
As though his deeds were gone from the earth,
   As though they had never been,-

And the only joy he found in the world
    From the whiskey cup he drew,
And when the wolves would howl in the night,
    Mad Tamahay would howl too.

Now Tamahay is stooped with age,
    His hair is white and shorn,
And no one there is to comfort his pains,-
    He is lonely and forlorn.

So deep in the woods, his cup in his hand,
    The sad old warrior raves,
And then with a tremor he breathes his last,-
    And dogs have found better graves.

Such was the death of Tamahay,
    And now his tale is sung,
Who lived many a bold and glorious year,
    But wanted to die young.

Anchises Holds the Babe Aeneas

Some unreflective prescience seems to gleam
In your new eyes, and guess the oracle,
That your days will be hard. Still I rejoice—
More than I ever gladdened over gold
And glory gained in battle—I rejoice
At this your quiet birth. How hard it is
To say what happiness it is to bear
A child to burdens, and give flesh a form
To endure the swords and iron of the foe,
And all the oceanic god can do
When goaded by his spiteful sister Hera,
Unless the truth of things lies not in strife,
Or tears, or chaos—any of fortune's works—
But in the strange deep influence that wells
Within man's heart, and overcomes all strife,
All tears, all chaos—all of fortune's works;
And maybe love, that seems to be as frail
As a week-old stalk, is after all more fierce
Than sea-spewed tempests, stronger even than war.

The Dream of Enkidu

(based on a passage from the Gilgamesh epic)

This is the story of how the vigorous friend
Of Gilgamesh in a vision presaged his end,
And how Shamash, the Lord of Day, the All-Perceiving,
Moved at the spectacle of his primal grieving,
Delivered him comforting words in a reverie.
It was that hour when the still austerity
Of nighttime weighs as thick as the plowman's yoke,
When Enkidu, the child of nature, awoke
And gazed around at a world grown newly foreign—
The trembling stars, the marsh, and the tangled warren
Of Uruk's streets where she lay on the sandy plain,
Were each infused by his agitated brain
With a desperate beauty, tinged with a vain desire,
As though he had never known these things with entire,
Consuming love until that unshrouded instant,
Though what was most reluctantly fair was the vigilant,
Apprehensive look on the face of the king,
Who sat by in the shadows, sadly wondering
At the sight of his friend's affliction, having been stirred
Out of his rest by the willess moans that he heard
Emerge from the warrior's throat in the throes of his dream.
Then Enkidu cried out with a sudden scream:
"My young and royal companion, my partner in war—
Do you know that we will not often meet, as before,
When we traveled the charted world together, and vied
With the gods, and the sons of the gods, by each other's side;
For I have witnessed strange visions in my repose:
The high gods in counsel, determined to chastise those

Who challenged their superintendence; I heard Enlil,
The master of men, declare his infallible will.
'Take one of these two,' he said, 'who dared to slay
The ward of the forests of Lebanon, and display
The trophied head of the bull that we set free
In the world of men to be the agency
Of our unreverenced strength—go, bear him away
To the halls where the sullen queen of the dead holds sway,
Where there is no striving, neither the victory
That cheers a man's heart in life, nor the eminency
Which he will endure a world of trouble to have.'
Then I imagined the doors of the musty grave
Were parted, and there emerged a monstrous shape—
A creature half-man, half-bird, with lips agape
And vacuous stare, and hands like an eagle's claws;
He said not a single word, but the evident cause
Of his coming to me was to bear me towards that abode
From which no man returns, at the end of that road
None travels twice. There the bodiless people sit
With dust for their drink, and brackish clay for their meat;
There old kinds have tossed away their futile crowns,
Old mighty kings, who once reigned over the towns
Of famous Sumer, with all the authority
Of Anu or Ki, and all the extravagancy
Of the gaudy sun-god, now inured to the toil
Of digging forever down in the fruitless soil,
As any common soul. Upon my arrival,
I was taken before the stansion of the archival
And cheerless goddess, Belit Sheri, who read
From an enormous tablet, then raised her head
To scan me impatiently before demanding
Of her bloodless, apparitional servants there standing:
'Who directed this one to come and dwell with us
In the house of the dead?' As cold and tremulous

I turned at these words as the traveler lost in the waste,
Or the citizen the merciless bailiff has cast
In the dank of the prison, yet soon as the goddess spoke
Her ominous greeting to me, in terror I woke."
Then the tameless monarch of Uruk, who kept his calm
The tale's distressing duration, pressed his palm
Against his flooding eyes, and gave way to a weeping
His weathered mind held hitherto in the keeping
Of regal self-possession, and fell to a heaving
That rocked his heroic frame, for here was a grieving
That could have no solace or remedy at his hands—
Could not be stemmed at its source by his commands—
And whatever else his valor could overcome,
He could do none else but watch his friend succumb
To death's more dominant force. Then Enkidu,
In desperate sorrow, and agitated all through,
Accosted the firmament with his lamentation:
"Was this the deliberate end of your creation,
Lord Anu, Lord Shamash? Was this the fate you foresaw
When you husbanded my life from the mud and the straw
In the soulless wilderness, to dissolve it again
Among the violence of forces blind and terrene,
Though not till I thought the full, embittering fact
Of this dissolution? Did you think I would contract
To accept a being on such preposterous grounds,
Or did you suppose the universe so abounds
In novelty and fairness, that it was worth
Such an afflicting knowledge to traverse the earth
Marveling at her impermanent loveliness?
I tell you it is not so, but sooner than bless
The distant day of my birth, I would have remained
Beneath the abiding silence, null and unpained
By the apprehension of what these dreams portend,
If I had known my life would have such an end.
I remember the work of this door, how we carried home

The load of lumber we spoiled from the fecund dome
Of Cedar Mountain, and how we set it in place,
And carved the lintel with figures of bearing and grace,
And hung the frame with our weathered arms, to attest
To the arduous fame we gained for ourselves in the west;
But now I perceive this proud exalted arch
Will serve but to usher the steps of the funeral march
That bears my intentionless corpse to its desuetude,
And I swear, I would have leveled that sacred wood
On the steep of Cedar Mountain, and burned each tree
In a pyre of devastation, before this should be.
And what of the Lady of Shamhat? She who conveyed
My steps from the brutish savannah, and allayed
The uncivil throes of my soul in an embrace
Lasting for an euphoric week, till the place
Of my birth had grown to a faltering reminisence,
And rising from this holy concupiscence,
Escorted my entry into the city wall
To interchange with men, and then through the hall
Of the unsurpassable king, my eventual mate;
And to lie on her body, and kiss her breasts, was a state
As magnificent as any fashioned thing
Elicited from chaos' old jostling
Has ever known or enjoyed, though not so sweet
To recompense the thought that we two will meet
No more in the carnal way, nor did the sight
Of her beautiful cheek on my arm suffice to requite
The anguish of forfeiting that beauty forever."
And when he had ranted thus, in the fit and the fever
Of hopeless dejection, the wound-stamped fighter exploded
Into a frenzy of tears, till his strength eroded
In the vehemence of his grief, and finally he wept
His spirit into exhaustion—then he slept.
And into the midst of his slumber stole the god—
Shamash, the high and resplendent king, at whose nod

The warrior once and his soul emerged from the sod.
He did not appear, though the man could tell he was there;
He did not speak, thought the other was quite aware
Of his mind's significance without that noise:
"Child Enkidu," he began, "why do you voice
Such terrible execrations against your birth?
When we husbanded your life from the thoughtless earth,
And opened your eyes with sight, and invested your days
With strife and attainment, did we in our minds not appraise
The transient good of this your devised estate
As a full and adequate reason to vindicate
Our mastery over the void, and was it not best
To have awakened to even the fleetingest
Of triumphs and pleasures, rather than languish still
In the chains of nothingness, and fail to fulfill
The least of your potency, not having been.
For only consider the lovely things you have seen
In the land of the living, how you have lain by the side
Of the gorgeous girl of the temple, and gratified
Your sight with the vision of her devested waist
Where she lay on the moonlit porch, and delected your taste
With kisses laid all over her passionate flesh;
And remember as well when you and Gilgamesh
Returned from the starry hills of Lebanon
With triumph and spoils, and bearing a gonfalon
Of your mighty enemy's arms, how the folk amassed
In the avenues of Uruk acclaimed as you past,
And swore that never a warrior could contend
With rivals as great as Enkidu and his friend.
Such memories I think should answer your urgent grief,
For when we decreed the forms of a mortal life,
It was our reasonable will, and our work, to endue
His days with a purposeful laboring after these two,
Glory and love, regarding their excellence
As a grace to be fairly had at any expense.

So weep no more for your fate, irascible child—
Since you were called to the world from the empty wild
You have had good things in your time, and when you depart,
Your regal friend, out of love and anguish of heart,
Will build for your bones a durable monument,
And gather the people often there to lament
The passing of one so brave, so your name will persist."
And when these words had their ending, the dormative mist
That covered the mournful mind of the warrior broke,
And seeing all things through pacified eyes, he awoke.

He gazed on the city, the seat of his earthly home,
And considered how fair was the sheen that played on the dome
Of the king's old palace, and what a fine domain
Was many-peopled Uruk; he noticed the plain
That stretched like a world before the messenger,
And also the stars of the night, how lovely they were.

Vera Paz

He ended his song, though the ceiba boughs
Still rung with the chords' last sweet vibration,
And staring from every painted face
Was a gaze of wonder and elation,
As though they just heard the delectable voice
Of Kinish or Chac, or the Lord of Creation.

Then all together they raised a plea,
These denizens of the land of war
And urged the stranger to start again
The delightful strain of his holy lore;
So the friar joyfully complied
And struck the teplanastle once more.

The melody spread over the hills,
Over the shade of their smoking crowns
And over the foliate valleys that fell
Like so many folds in a verdant gown
Wrapped round the earth, where the cedar and oak
Quivered with the appeal of the tone;

It stirred the quetzal high in the roof
Proudly displaying its various hues
Above a lightless jungle, where snakes
Devise their traps, and the leopard pursues
Its nighttime game, and the jaguar predates
Alone in groves where the orchids profuse.

Nor less did that novel music resound
In the ruined habitations of man—
Mid the empty villages that skirt
The silent coast of Atitlan,
Or where horrific deities took
Imbued devotions in old Copan;

And it resonated the vines that bound
The murals of Nakbe's littered hall;
Wound the significant altars that topped
The vicious temples of proud Tikal,
And covered the place where, masked in jade,
Lay the king of Palenque, the Lord Pakal.

Then the Friar lifted his voice to sing
Of the making of earth, in order to please
The loving mind of Almighty God,
And how, to cleanse our iniquities
His Son descended and suffered here-
And the words of his marvelous song were these:

"Look at this sacred tree—with what life
Its burgeoning branches effloresce,
And what an abundance of natural kinds
Dwell in its canopy's green excess,
And consider that this extravagance
Grows from the depths of nothingness.

Likewise, consider the harpy bird,
The king of the skies, quite overjoyed
In the force of his huge form, when he soars
In his arrogant way, on thunders buoyed,
And remember that every flight he takes
Sets out from the pre-existent void.

All things that have their being here
Once had no being at all—therefore
He alone is God who has the strength
To summon the world from naught, and assure
Its fragile endurance from hour to hour—
He alone is fit to serve and adore.

And as he fashions uncompelled,
Nor out of any malignancy
(Since evil or bound's no God at all),
His work is pure gratuity,
Effect of the only adequate cause—
A superabundance of charity.

Then since the one who called use here
Was moved by love in all he achieved
It follows that his essential law
Is to give to others as we received
And show our neighbor that very love
In which ourselves were first conceived.

But now consider the race of men,
How villainous they were from the first,
Being envious, and covetous,
Proud, insubordinate, and perverse,
Without affection or understanding,
And ever to heaven's will adverse;

Defiling the face of the earth with their deeds,
The fruits of deceit and incontinence—
Murder and rape, and the breaking of vows,
And the stir of continual variance,
In every one of their merciless acts
Impelled by the lust for dominance.

Therefore, they justly incurred the sting
Of death as the wage for their terrible sin,
Since they in their violence would not concur
With the gracious scheme of their sovereign,
Nor cede their souls to that furious love
In which they have had their origin.

But God is not checked in his righteous ends,
Nor will he allow man's ancient treason
To frustrate his own benevolence—
So he sent his Son, the eternal reason
And mirror of his own supernal will,
To dwell with our wayward tribe for a season.

He taught us the creed of perfect love—
To bless our foe as well as our friend,
To forbear in patience our neighbor's faults
As the Lord forbears us where we offend,
And to recall to our mind always
How far above earth is our final end.

But for all that his life was innocent,
His works replete with sanctity,
They raged against his word, and smeared
His teaching with every calumny,
Until at last they abducted him
And nailed him to a cross-wise tree.

Still God would accomplish his own intent,
So he granted the Son his manumission
From the thrall of death, and raised him up,
To verify his divine commission,
And witness that neither sin nor death
Would keep his work from its last fruition.

Therefore I declare to you the hour
Of sacrifice is over and gone,
For what in your sin can you perform
More pleasing than what the Lord has done;
What offer to the King of Heaven
More valuable than his perfect Son.

And know that the shedding of precious blood
Delights not our God, who once infused
That vital liquid in every vein,
And rather rejoices as each is used
After its inwrought excellence,
And not as its life is lost and abused.

The sole oblation our Lord will take
Is a heart contrite, and consecrate
To the love that moves the suns and the stars,
Content in all ways to imitate
Our Savior when he lived in the flesh
And shared the pain of our lost estate.

So have no more to do with the fiends
You have served so long to your detriment,
Or with their red and hideous rites;
But turn your hearts instead, and repent,
Assured of finding the boundless grace
That flows from the one omnipotent."

Then when the Friar had ended again,
The astounded chief stood up in the midst,
And taking his well-worn ax in hand,
He crossed to a grotto opposite
Where the shrine of the tribal deity stood,
And smashed the thing to a thousand bits.

Nor did he relent just then, but struck
Till he made ten shards of every shard,
And the power of the idol died in the dirt
Where the bones of his victims lay interred,
While the mass of his people gathered there
Marveled at all they saw and had heard.

The Wreckers of Kerry

They rowed beyond the cluttered rocks
    That loomed like a palisade,
And past the rush of the breaking tide,
    To scan the wreck they made.

There was no light but for the lamp
    That hung on their weathered boom,
And by its treacherous glow they steered
    About the heaving gloom,

And caught the sight of drowned men
    Whose cold and swollen flanks
Bobbed on the eerily gasping waves
    Amid the shattered planks.

But mindless of this testament
    To their own iniquity
Those wreckers pulled at a massive chest
    That floated on the sea,

When a rogue and violent wave emerged
    Out of the mischievous night
And beat their boat on the very rocks
    Where the other ship had split,

And dragged each one of those murderous souls
    To a death such as they planned
For other men when they lit the way
    Towards the unharbored land.

Now who can say, and speak for sure,
 Just by what arcane laws
The waters moved, or to what realm
 Referred the final cause;

Whether the exacerbated heavens
 Destroyed those miscreants,
Or whether it was the fair effect
 Of brutal happenstance.

So much we know without a doubt
 Of the wrecker's proper grave—
There was an awesome righteousness
 Abiding in that wave.

The Testament

Heiligenstadt, October 6ᵗʰ, 1802

You men who account me spiteful or stubborn or proud,
Or out of some hatred of man, aloof from the crowd,
How greatly you wrong me, failing to comprehend
The secret cause of those manners which so offend.
Since I was a child, I have felt my ardent mind
Suffused with goodwill, nor was I disinclined
To achieve great things, which I strove for endlessly;
But for six years now, from a hopeless malady
I have suffered, compelled to confess to myself at last
That no cure is at hand, that the terrible years which have past
But prelude a tedious life thus afflicted and lonely,
Though formed for the love of fellowship. And if only
I could hide from my perverse troubles, but always the sense
Of my deprivation returns with violence
Whenever I mix among the oblivious crowd.
Yet how could I plead for myself, and say, "Speak aloud,
Shout, for now I am deaf?" How confess a blight
In that sense which I once possessed at such a height
As few men, living or dead, have ever known,
And which should be perfect in me? Oh, how could I own
That fortune had thus made such a fool of me!
I cannot do it—therefore, for charity
Forgive me whenever I seem to draw away,
For sorrow on sorrow it is that men should say
He is bitter or arrogant because I behave
In this cryptic manner, though truly, nothing I crave
So much as companionship, the civil delight

Of intimate talks that last well into the night,
And only the stroke of senseless circumstance
Has driven me to this seeming petulance
And left me banished from men, compelled to abjure
The pleasure of company, condemned to endure
A torment of mind both singular and cruel.
Once when I walked the rolling roads of Nemuhl
A friend who was by bid me attend to the chant
Of some idle shepherd, how sweet and exuberant
It rose from the glen on the noon-warm zephyr that stirred
The leaves on the laurel tree—yet nothing I heard
Of the peasant's carefree tune, or the natural sigh
Of those victorious trees as the winds passed by,
And I only wept and stared desperately at my friend
Who stood wondering by, unable to comprehend.
Such bitter moments as these, as they grew less rare,
Had driven me quite to the precipice of despair,
And a little more—well, I dare not say what had been,
For only think of the monstrous plight I was in;
Graced with the mastery to forge the substance of sound
After the longing of men, to please and astound,
Whether I fashioned for keyboard some delicate air
That falls on the satisfied mind as placid and fair
As the light of the moon, or whether I summoned the voice
Of a hundred tongues in praise of the bountiful joys
We have in our being, until the hearkening soul,
Transported beyond the pulsing aureole
Of the reverent sun, treads on the stars as on stones,
And the universe seems his to command at my tones;
So it wasn't presumption or folly which led me to deem
Those talents devolved to my part from a beauty supreme,
To be exercised in accord with the heavenly will—
And then to discover the flourishing of that skill
Frustrated by this, the most inane of afflictions,

As though our Lord, by the greatest of contradictions,
Impeded the duties established by His own word.
I was lost, and could make no sense of a lot so absurd,
And began to consider death as a preferable state
To a life tormented by this ridiculous fate.
It was only my art that saved me, for then I swore
I would never quit this wretched existence before
I brought forth all of the surging music inside me,
In spite of whatever circumstance defied me,
In spite of whatever ailments affronted this frame,
In spite of the fury of all the forces that aim
At man and his happiness in our broken sphere.
Thus am I compelled, in the twenty-eighth sad year
Of my pitiable life to turn philosopher
And choose patience to guide me henceforth—so may I endure
In this frowning resolve till Atropos' fine blade
Sever the thread and my empty husk is laid
In the tomb's appropriate silence. Till then I persist
In my role as nature's defiant melodist,
To make the world resound with the beautiful clamor
Of my soul's relentless thunder, to acquaint and enamor
All human hearts with what is most lovely and good
In the human realm, and most worthy to be pursued,
To redeem a world too often hideous
By the grace of pure and abundant loveliness,
Consoling mortals the breadth of their tenuous span,
For this, to my mind, appears the best part of man.
My fellow creatures, whoever might peruse
This lamentable correspondence, do not refuse
Your compassion to one so strangely suffering,
One whose heart is filled with goodwill, as the mighty king
Of this universe can attest, one who has striven

With all of the talent and all of the might he was given,
Against the infirmities that fell to his part,
To assume a place among honorable workers of art.
Do no forget me after my days are through,
For while I was here, I labored always for you
Despite my manifold sorrows, and also, please know
How I wished to make you happy—therefore, be so.

The Victory at Quito

Down the mountain pass to Quijos
    In the quarter of the north,
The captain Benalcazar
    And his squad came rushing forth,
With their old world armor gleaming
    Down the length of their hot train,
And their snapping flags declaring
    All the pride of martial Spain.

And before them Ruminavi
    Fled alone along the path
From the ever-nearing clamor
    Of his foes' impending wrath;
And his limbs were faint and trembling
    From the labors he had born,
And his feet were raw and bleeding
    From wounds the rocks had torn.

Still the liege of Atahualpa
    Persisted as he could,
And still the regal Spanish
    Thundered through the wood,
Till they gained a florid clearing
    In their fierce celerity
Where they found the warrior leaning
    On a lonely boxwood tree.

And they set at once upon him
　　With a great triumphant shout,
And they dragged him off to Quito
　　Where the flames had not gone out;
Then they threw him in their prison
　　Bound fast as any beast,
And retired to their quarters
　　For the revel and the feast.

And when morning light in Quito
　　Peaked from the hills once more
The captain Benalcazar
　　Stood at the prison door;
And he strode into the chamber
　　With an air of high disdain
And sneered down on his captive
　　Who slept upon his chain.

Then he kicked him in his fury
　　And spit upon his head,
And demanded all the lucre
　　That his heart so coveted;
But noble Ruminavi
　　Said not a word at all,
And only sat serenely
　　Against the granite wall.

So fuming Benalcazar
        With a flourish of his hand
Urged on some rock-browed soldiers
        Who stood at his command;
And they seized the famous general
        Who they then began to beat
With the flat side of their sabers,
        With their fists, and with their feet.

But the lord Ruminavi,
        For all that they could do,
Had not a word of riches
        To give that frantic crew;
So then frowning Benalcazar
        Turned sharply to depart
With the white heat of his anger
        Searing at his heart.

The august and warlike condor
        Had soared against the noon;
The furtive owl had chanted
        To the forest-gilding moon;
And when the yawning morning
        Had stirred the town once more,
The captain Benalcazar
        Stood at the prison door.

He demanded all the jewels
        From the Incas' ancient hoard,
But the lord Ruminavi,
        He answered not a word;
So the Spaniard took a torchlight
        And burned his captive's feet
Till the flesh was all but swallowed
        By the devouring heat.

But for all the wicked torments
    That his captors could impose
The noble Ruminavi
    Only smiled at his foes,
And so thwarted Benalcazar
    With a curse and with a scowl
Pushed through his wondering soldiers
    And departed from the gaol.

The sleek and sable puma
    Had gone hunting through the shade;
The viper long had slumbered
    In the fatal nest he made;
And when again the morning
    Flumed through the valley floor
The captain Benalcazar
    Stood at the prison door.

Then he strode across the dungeon
    With a fixed impatient air
Until he stood astraddle
    His passive prisoner,
And with eyes all red and glaring,
    And beard all flecked with spray,
He demanded of his captive
    Where the Inca treasure lay.

"I have come here Ruminavi
    One final time to know
Where the fabled wealth of Quito
    Your dirty minions stow;
And I swear by all the power
    That my greater gods display
If you cross my will this last time
    You will surely die today.

Distant Lands and Near

The streets of Cajamarca
    Where your barbarous pomp has been
Are obstructed with the corpses
    Of the Incas' bravest men,
And your lord Atahualpa,
    Whom they used to hold in dread,
Now dons his royal tassle
    In the kingdom of the dead.

The palaces of Cuzco
    And the fat of Jauja's lands,
At once alike are gathered
    In the Spaniard's stronger hands,
And the hour is quickly coming,
    Before many years are through,
When San Jago's holy standard
    Will fly over all Peru.

So now the time is proper
    For the viceroy of the north
To accept the iron status
    Of matters going forth;
For fortune is a tyrant
    Whom we must accommodate—
So all wise men acknowledge
    Whether soon or late."

Then noble Ruminavi
    Who all this time sat by
In a long disdainful silence
    At last made his reply,
As his chest grew broad in anger,
    And his chin grew tense in spite,
And his voice rebounded loudly
    Like one mindless of his plight.

"If my lord Atahualpa
        Now lies sepulchered,
It is only since he trusted
        Too mildly to your word,
And that bent of royal honor
        Proved greatly to his cost—
But the profit of your treachery
        Is a shameful thing to boast.

It is true your shining army
        Has brought us many harms,
And carried half the empire
        Before your novel arms;
But in this I find no reason
        To do homage to your king—
The decrees of chance and justice
        Have never been one thing.

Once the sun's resplendent children
        With their golden staff in hand
Left the quiet vale of Tampu
        To sojourn in our land,
And to guide the wayward Inca
        To their father's perfect will,
So their place among the nations
        They could at last fulfill.

They taught the love of duty,
        And the prize of fortitude,
And the cost that every zinchi
        Owes to the general good;
So as Viracocha willed it
        In our dawn-elated prime,
So shall Ruminavi follow
        Even in this waning time."

Then the soldiers came and bound him
    With rigid cord and mesh
That bore in their hard fastness
    Into his naked flesh;
And they dumped him in a wagon
    And pulled him to the square
Where the smoke of devastation
    Still hung heavy in the air.

And before him Benalcazar
    Sat on a pilfered throne
That some Inca hand had fashioned
    From the timeless Andes' stone;
And his face twitched with the fever
    Of the fierce expectancy
Of destroying the one object
    Of his fear and enmity.

But noble Ruminavi,
    Like one without a care,
Fixed his eyes upon the captain's,
    And returned a placid stare;
As they led him up the scaffold
    And tied him to his place,
That expression of indifference
    Never left his face.

Then they killed the Incas' general—
    With the garrote in their fists
They extinguished his defiance
    With a few deliberate twists,
And when the silent warrior
    Seemed to cough his final breath
Two Spaniards came and struck him
    To be certain of his death.

Then they took his naked body
    And cast it in the street,
Where forsaken dogs were prowling
    In search of food to eat;
And captain Benalcazar
    With this soldiers all around
Took up their happy standards
    And marched proudly from the town.

The Dream of Abbie Burgess

Is that the noise of the agonized sea,
    That roars at my window-pane?
Is that the bawl of the northeast gale
    That bears the wreck and the rain?

And is that the boom of the iron coast
    Fronting the wild white crest
That even in this, my final bed,
    Permits me little rest?

Just such a storm comes back to me
    On the tide of memory
As ambushed Matinicus Rock
    Where she sits in the gleaming sea.

To Rockland father had sailed away,
    And mother and sister and I
Alone in the tower endured the wrath
    That blew about the sky.

The waves in their fury breached the walls
    And across the island rolled
Till not one stone on another stood
    Except for our ancient hold.

But with the ships in the unfed deep
Was all my thought and care,
For not a man aboard but lived
In our lamp's abiding glare.

Cloud-ward on the waves they surged,
And my heart rose with the crew;
Down into the trough they plunged
And all my heart fell too!

So desperately, in dusk and dark,
I tended to the light
Lest even the poorest cabin boy
Should perish in the night;

Lest even the smallest schooner boat
Should tumble in the gale
I labored at my heavy task
In terror I should fail.

Once when the ocean skirt the coop
I ran into the storm
And bore the frantic chickens back
In a basket on my arm.

Oh how I longed to gather in
Each man upon the sea
And bear him in my arms away
From its cold ferocity;

To bear him in my arms away
From the agitated swell
And place him on a solid coast
Where all things would be well.

Last night I dreamed of the weathered tower
    And in my dream it stood
Lonely amid the mounting tide
    In dark decrepitude.

The clouds that augur storm and rain
    Had mustered in the east;
The lightning whipped the champing waves,
    And the goading wind increased;

And homeward from the teeming banks
    Road many a lovely ship
And one by one each fell into
    The storm's remorseless grip.

Just at that moment every man
    To my mind did appear
Like the sleeping face of one beloved-
    Fragile, unique, and dear;

Or like the weeping of a child
    By thunder peals distressed,
Whom we to soothe at once enfold
    And clasp against our breast;

And all the world was like a gate
    Where ruin ever pressed,
And none but I was there to hold
    Its straining latches fast.

I hurried where the lighthouse stood,
    Just how I cannot tell,
But underneath my powerless feet
    The ocean rose and fell.

I seemed to float across the waves
Like a ghostly charioteer,
And as I went I watched all things
With trembling and with fear.

The night was stealing through the sky,
The tempest barked and raved,
And I must light the mouldering lamp
So all those might be saved.

Oh, who will keep the lighthouse flame
When I have fallen asleep?
And who will guard the noble souls
That travail in the deep?

And who will be the light from home
When their boats are tossed and staved,
And the monstrous ocean mounts with rage,
So all at last are saved?

A Sumerian Legend

The sun that rose in Kish for many hours
Had seered the walls that ringed the royal quad,
And burned the timeless rituals on the towers,
Imprinted in the dessicated sod
In olden days, to appease some arcane god.

Unsheltered from that painful radiance
Lay regal Nansin—or her remnant clay—
Provided every rich appertunance
That eases souls on their reluctant way
Into the kingdom of unwaking day.

And there beside her Lugalbanda sat,
Her lord and husband, just beyond the peaks
Of the unrelieving shade of the ziggurat,
Dispensing from the tears that washed his cheeks
The only rain that place had known for weeks.

Then suddenly, before the broken king
Appeared the gods, to offer consolation—
Terrestial Ki, the queen of flourishing,
And her consort in mankind's adoration,
Enlil, the lord of ruin and creation.

But the monarch was not pleased to see them there;
He only said, "I see how vain it was
To honor your sacrarium's with prayer
And sacrifice, and keep your arduous laws,
Since you have proved indifferent to my cause."

To which Enlil replied, "Though now you rue
The loss you have of death's persistent blight,
Later will come a time, when time is through,
When she will be restored to your new sight,
And walk by you in fields of perfect light."

And thus the king: "There cannot rise a dawn
So lustrous in its early glimmering;
There cannot grow a flower on the lawn
So lovely in its splendid burgeoning
Which could redeem the outrage of this thing."

And thus the god: "You speak as men must speak
Who lack the vision of the promised end,
And thus cannot account for the unique
And holy recompense that we intend,
But in the later days you will comprehend."

Once more the monarch answered to the god:
"Most certainly I speak as men must speak,
And understand as such a wretched clod
As you have fashioned, ignorant and weak,
Must understand the truth we mortals seek.

I only know that since your mastery
Is unassailable and infinite,
There's not a single sad calamity
But falls as your almighty wills permit,
Which out of righteousness might stymie it.

Look there—deprived of all her lively grace,
As cold and pallid as the stone she lies,
And if you thought it wrong death should efface
The beauty in the sweetest pair of eyes
That ever smiled, this would be otherwise.

So now I want none of your consolation,
In this world or in one to be prepared,
You did not exercise your domination
The hour my love and her goodness were ensnared-
And who can comfort pains he might have spared?"

This said, then Lugulbanda like one vexed
Rose and departed through the palace way—
Enlil observed his going, much perplexed,
And florid Ki, struck with a new dismay,
Fumbled the flowers from her rich bouquet.

Langston Blee

It was a low and a humid night
    By the bay of Barnegat,
Where the orange and the purple sun
    Behind the country set;

And there along the knotted pier
    The sailor Langston Blee
Walked slowly towards his little boat
    To ride upon the bay.

His ragged beard was flecked with gray,
    As the winter wave with foam,
And his blue coat wreaked of the sea
    That was his ancient home.

He scanned with a careful glance along
    The margin of the sea,
Where churning billows lift their heads
    To the sky perpetually;

There he espied the heavy clouds
    That roll about the moon,
And in his heart he knew too well
    That a storm was coming soon.

Now running down the knotted pier
    Came the wife of Langston Blee,
Where he unmoored his little boat
    To ride upon the bay.

She pleaded with him not to go;
    She said the task could wait;
She told him if he drowned that night
    She could not bear her fate.

But her husband could not watch her tears;
    He only turned away,
And said he'd moor again before
    The first pink light of day.

Now Langston Blee's set out to sea;
    Now he's sunk below the line,
When the thunder gathered in the sky,
    And the winds began to whine—

And the ocean raised her ragged head
    Out of the churning bars,
And seemed like one enraged to scream
    At the storm-shrouded stars.

For hours that night it stormed at sea,
    For hours upon the bay,
For hours upon the coast where sat
    The wife of Langston Blee;

Until the thunder's wrath was cooled,
    The lightning's heat was spent,
And the dissolving clouds revealed
    The starry firmament,

Where the yawning constellations
　　Through the silent void are cast,
Hurled with that same speed they gained
　　At the primeval blast,

And never is heard a sound or voice
　　Through all that infinite span,-
Not the crashings of the angered sea,
　　Not the tears of sorrowing man.

Langston Blee did not come that night,
　　Nor at dawn to the bay,
Though his wife stood waiting by the shore,
　　In the first pink light of day.

She stood alone and searched the sea
　　As far as her eye could scan,
But all that came was the rolling tide
　　That was since the world began.

Daniel Carnagon

They lay him on the stone-worked floor,
Three casual soldiers, then they turned,
As beings wholly unconcerned,
And ambled out the clashing door.

It was November, and the walls
Vibrated with the hardened rain
That whips the granite coast of Maine
When March brings in its standard squalls.

The family stood in a sullen poise
And heard his labored respiration,
And strained to catch the sad relation
Heaved on the breath of his failing voice:

"Hear me a moment, for my contrition,
Since now my life is like those grains
Scattered by inefficient rains
To a bare clay, without fruition.

I was a child of England's moors-
Reared by the Humber's level banks,
By a father filled with pious thanks
And a mother sweet as new-cut flowers.

I had each blessing that a child
Needs for his life's felicity
In their exhaustless charity—
But I was malcontent and wild.

So when I came to means, I went
And threw in with a worthless set,
Until a deep and deadly debt
Forced me to join the regiment,

Which soon shipped out for this strange nation
To fight with men we did not hate—
And when my mother learned my fate
She wasted in her tribulation.

And my poor father, drear and friendless,
Was left to live his barren days
Puzzling at heaven's searchless ways,
And bearing a remorse that's endless.

Much greater were his misery
Were he by now to see the child
Who as a babe he held, and smiled,
And wondered what his life would be."

He ended here, and then he tried
To force the arduous coming air
Into the sound of a soothing prayer,
But before three lines were spoke, he died.

Then the menfolk took their tools of toil
And strode into the adverse gale
To find a place they could prevail
With labor on the igneous soil;

There in a grave not deep or wide
They lay the soldier's shrouded form,
Just sheltered from the icy storm
And the violence of the saline tide.

Elegy for the Poet's Father, Dr. Anthony Signorelli

After your rites of mourning had been fulfilled,
My father, and the reluctant fact instilled
Of your enduring absence within my heart,
I took a volume of yours, and sat apart
To stare at the vacant, petrified remains—
The robust thrones of inaccessible brains—
From what were men, or such as seemed like men;
And I considered how time and its discipline
Joined you forever to those unthought durations,
The vast eons of death, and the oblivious nations
That have arisen, reveled in the mirth
Of their momentary being, then passed from the earth:
The proto-humans of Afar, whose pithecine eyes
Once adumbrated the first and the faintest surmise
Of their brutal end, as they tread an upright course
Through the ash of Laetoli, and also, those masters of force,
Battering stone implements in a flake-strewn forge,
Where they preyed and were preyed upon in the heart of the gorge
At flowering Olduvai, and the first of our kind,
Who washed in the Omo's dark waters, with fledgling mind
Perturbed by what lay in the shapes of the firmament,
And what lay beyond, or that tribe of arcane descent
Who dwelt among the surety of sullen caves
In the quiet vale of Neander, adorning the graves
Of fostered kin with the yarrow flowers they culled,
The initial testament of grief in a world
That would after burst with it. And when the millions of years

Have dissipated again which ushered those peers
In the aimless pageant—indeed, when tenfold a span
Has come and gone by in the tenebrous passage of man—
You'll come not again; your lesser universe,
Annihilated by life's abiding curse,
No epoch will heal, no generations restore
To integrity, so long as this frame perdure
Beneath the dominion of time and longing. Still I,
Irreconciled to a fate I could not defy,
Contend with death in the only manner I may
By preserving the memory of what you were from decay,
As I could not your body, and amid long ruination
Erecting an everlasting protestation
Against your perishing, certain of this,
That whatever else the loathsome metastasis
Of mutinous nature could violate and confound,
It ought not have done so to you, who was so sound,
So moderate in judgment, so generous a friend,
Such a lover of lovely things, who could apprehend
In the least of beauty's fugitive visitations
Among your quiet days, the sufficient occasion
For perfect delight, whose lifelong study it was
To comprehend the genuine springs and the laws
Of human striving, with ever unbittered mind
Considering what baseness was there to find
In the welter of motivation, behind the mask
Of our custom and proper speech—a difficult task.
Little the waning age could spare such a man.
Now you have returned to that void from which you began,
Oblivious to all the goodness that thrives
In our sweet world—to the elemental joy that revives
At the rise of each day, the inscrutable ecstasy
Of embodied being that births the melody
Of a thousand songs, such as you loved to hear.

Nor will the mass of our delirious sphere
Fail to repay that very indifference,
But he who has laughed, will laugh; who has danced, will dance,
And he who has been consumed by some veiled ambition
Will struggle still to bring it at length to fruition,
Quite as if there was never such a catastrophe
As the dignified person you were, ceasing to be.
But what is most sad is that I, your only son,
Having wept the appointed season, must carry on
And live henceforth as though you had not been,
Taking a hand in marriage, watching the scene
Of the novel soul stir in my child's first motions,
While you remain like the earth. Nor can my devotions
Alter the merest moment of the iron past
When we quarelled, and the greater part of the blame was cast
On myself, as I know, or how I failed to attain
Any prominence in life and affairs, and gain
Your valued esteem, such as every son aspires
To have of his father, and every father desires
To bear towards his son, since I was born with the art
Of fashioning language after the frame of the heart,
And regarded the work of its perfect consummation
A glorious endeavor, since never an eminent nation
But revered the skill of matching wisdom to rhymes—
But a poet gets no honor in these times.
For these things there is no adequate remedy,
No truth of our realm that soothes the cruelty,
Or helps us to understand it after our ways,
But the evil of it persists till the end of days;
And God forbid I insult your memory
By taking comfort in easy falsity
When all should be sorrow, protest, and lamentation.
Still, I think I have cause for honest consolation
When I reflect on all you have left to me-
Not merely the pattern of flesh, but the legacy

Of intellectual fervor that was the prime thing
In your earthly character, that famishing
After the knowledge of full and final truth
Which I caught of your emulation in my youth,
And from which I trust I will never suffer divorce
Till the last and the feeblest hour of my physical course,
But keep with me, in spite of age and despair
This treasure, and finest fruit of a father's care.
And so I perceive this marvel of human existence,
Which but for its transient state, and the helpless persistence
Of parasitical woe, we might be deceived
To take for the paradise so long bereaved—
A fragile garden, abounding and crystalline—
We know it not in itself, not its origin
In the pre-material deliberation,
Nor what is the last fruition of creation
To be in the harvest of eternity,
But each of us lives an incorrigible mystery,
Forever mired in final ignorance
Of our experience authentic significance,
Forever disturbed by hopes of transcendent worth.
And as obscure as the moment of our birth
Is the moment of our death—I cannot declare
With the least assurance what truly happened there
In the darkness before morning, when the distress
Of your affliction that raged beneath my caress
Conquered the vital springs, and the ashen tone
Invaded your limbs, and in the room alone
I wept tears as violent as ineffectual;
Nor can I guess in what shadow lands you dwell,
Nor in what form or mode incorporal
You continue your wonted being, or if at all.
But like all men here, I catch fleeting auguries
Of unearthly ends, and changeless verities
In the human constitution, and also I sense,

With the perfect warrant of normal sapience,
How insufficient is matter, and all of these things
Bear an intimation of different reckonings,
And suggest that what transpired in that hideous night
Awaits its proper account, that one may requite
Our souls for what they endure in our mortal day,
That nothing good is wholly thrown away,
That the judgment together shall time and death remove,
And life's last word shall be accorded to love.
So much we have for wisdom in this world,
So much I am content with—from nothingness hurled
Into this state of startling contingency,
Where the best of things to our minds is charity,
I cast my lot with the more illustrious hope.
Henceforth I live as one whose aims have scope
Beyond the evident realm, and the imperfect merits
That crown the common labor; one who inherits
A patrimony in death, thus satisfied
To know my rueful impermanence, and abide
The ineluctable moment when it appears;
And one who will hold, till the last of my unknown years,
Your memory in reverence and gratitude,
And harbor the faith, however much it elude
The adequacy of thought, that I've not said
The last of farewells to you, but that it is laid
In the fullness of time to sit by you again-
After the vanity and the passions of men-
When we wake together beneath ineffable skies
To see ourselves at last with altered eyes,
But hearts with all the accustomed love astir,
And weep for the sorrows of our lives that were.

The Monk by the Sea

A monk lived by the sea—
He walked along the sand,
He wandered silently
Without a friend at hand,

And when the last gray swatch
Of day hung in the sky,
He'd wander there and watch
The ships go sailing by;

And sometimes it would happen
When winter storms would blow,
Some rash and foolish captain
Would bring his ship to woe;

And the monk would see the boat
That floundered in the tide,
And he would hear the shout
The desperate sailors cried,

And helpless to give aid
In the black and icy shoals,
To the Lord God he prayed
For mercy on their souls.

I too have walked alone
Along that very strand,
And heard the ocean groan
When winter was at hand,

And seen the gray sky lit
With the sun's last waning rays,
And thought a little bit
On the ever-darkening days-

On the vileness and the hate,
The chaos and the rage,
And all the sins that weight
The sinking of the age;

And finding myself frail
To rescue humankind,
To Him behind the veil
I've raised my faltering mind

And sadly lingering there
Where the dying current curled,
I have prayed a little prayer
For the shipwreck of the world.

Song of the Wandering Poet

Among the meadow's bright alleys,
　　Where the violets savor the shade,
And the thrush in the wet thicket dallies,
　　And the deer runs loose in the glade,
I wander the field solitary,
　　As light as the wind in its way,
And with my own song made merry,
　　I go signifying all day.

So when noon in the sky is blazing
　　Above a world halcyon,
My joyful strain I go raising
　　To laud the lustrous sun;
And when eve's white luminary
　　Spreads out its nebulous light,
The theme of my music I vary
　　And sing the beauty of night.

For a lightsome harp my soul is
　　On which Nature plays the chords,
And with her all the control is
　　Over my feelings and my words;
And since God was pleased to have fashioned
　　My soul in such a way,
With love and praise impassioned
　　I sing His goodness all day.

So I fly where the lily is springing,
  And the iris stands unfurled,
For the world never minded my singing,
  So I never minded the world;
And all the days of my roaming,
  This only desire I keep,
To hymn a song in the gloaming
  Awhile, and then fall asleep.

About the Author

———∿∿∘ଚ୧ଓ୦୧ଚ∘∿∿———

Mark Anthony Signorelli is a poet, playwright, and essayist. His work can be found at markanthonysignorelli.com.